THE SHOT DOCTOR

THE SHOT DOCTOR

Nothin' But Net

Leroy McClure Jr.

Copyright © 2015 Authored By Leroy McClure Jr.

All rights reserved.

ISBN: 1508964637
ISBN 13: 9781508964636

Dedication

I dedicate this book to all of the student athletes who I have worked with in my twenty-five-plus years of being a professional educator. I would like to give special props and thanks to the graduating high-school class of 2015 for their hard work, dedication, commitment, and love of the game of basketball. May your hard work continue to pay dividends and increase your "net" worth in your future endeavors.

The Shot Doctor's Golden Nuggets

Leroy McClure Jr., also known as Coach McClure, says:

Think. Choose. Do. The strategy for the game of life.™

No excuses. No explanations. High execution and high expectation. Just get the job done!

I believe in teaching children how to:

- turn problems into opportunities
- turn adversities into victories
- become winners even in losing situations

We must get our athletes to reset the standards by excelling in attitude and academics.

Triple A Academy stands for attitude, academics, and athletics, in that order.

He would love to see a student athlete as a valedictorian or salutatorian.

Some people have much on display but nothing in the warehouse.

No matter what is going on in your life, "all things work together for the good of those who love Him and are called according to His purpose." Romans 8:28

Acknowledgments

- Coach Tim Singleton, an outstanding point guard from Notre Dame, and his son, Tyler, helped to shape the basketball program at Triple A Academy. His coaching of the team and his son's talent made our basketball program excellent. When I asked him to coach my son, he said yes. This allowed me to focus more time on building our organization. It was the beginning of us building an excellent, world-class athletic program with the Triple A Stallions Amateur Athletic Union (AAU) program and later the great educational institution at Triple A Academy for student athletes on and off the court.
- Coach Robert Washington, a new Triple A Academy assistant varsity coach, believed in my shooting abilities and saw how the fruit fell greater from a nourished, watered, and well-tended tree.
- Richland College Men's Basketball Coach Louis Stone gave me an opportunity to display my shooting abilities and encouraged me to continue my education. Coach Stone was very adamant about me teaching my son to master the mid-range shot so he could become the best.
- We were blessed by the Texas Titans Team, a world-class organization, because of their faith lived through character-building workshops, player devotional periods, encouraging

words, the team chaplain, and much, much more. I want to thank Kenny and Lisa Trout for allowing my son, King, to not only play for the Titans but to compete on the most competitive platform in the country. This enabled King to hone his skills and display the fruits of the spirit nationwide.

Foreword

If the communities of our future are to be peaceful, sage, and productive, it calls for far greater tolerance, understanding, and sharing among many varied individuals.

In 1996, I met one such individual, Leroy McClure Jr. He was a man on a mission determined to give more opportunity for youth to improve their reading, go to college, and fulfill their dreams as professional doctors, lawyers, athletes, and much more. I watched a vibrant, energetic, and God-fearing man live what he believed. He spoke to countless parents, business leaders, legislators, and anyone who would listen about the crisis of illiteracy in the African American community. He reached many youth through basketball because he learned to read as he turned the pages in books and magazines with stories about athletes. Leroy said this so much: "I teach people how to turn problems into opportunities, how to turn adversities into victories, and how to become winners even in losing situations."

His beliefs did not just stop as an expression of thought. He took his knowledge and skills of reading and basketball to high-crime communities in the Dallas–Fort Worth metropolitan areas. He is still living his life full of passion to eradicate illiteracy while training athletes in the game that he played and loved. A year ago, Leroy had to stop playing recreational basketball because he hurt his Achilles tendon when he went to dunk the basketball. While this may have sidelined his physical play, he began to rely on his mental ability. A new vision was birth with our son, King. We begged King to diversify his basketball game by shooting the ball more. However, King suffered a minor injury, too. As he sat out from some key games, he began to reflect on his basketball career. Based on my husband's experiences with injuries, he told King that this was a "minor setback for a major comeback." King was all ears as his dad talked to him about the art of shooting. I began to see an even closer bond between a father and a son.

This bond between my husband and my son is a mother's dream. We give all praise, glory, and honor to God for allowing us to see how "children are a heritage from the Lord. The fruit of the womb is a reward." We really see firsthand that children are indeed "like arrows in the hands of a warrior" as King David wrote in Psalm 127:3–5. The short time that my husband has worked with King to become an efficient shooter speaks to not only a man on a mission, but one that is a positive influence, starting at home with his own son.

My husband and my son have accomplished much on and off the court. I am grateful that they recognize that all good and perfect gifts come from above. Both of these men have gained much respect from me and the rest of our family members. May this book bless many families and athletes and may it make a difference in their lives.

—Yvette McClure, wife and writer

Preface

The game is on the line. You were fouled with three seconds left in the game. You have the chance to win the basketball game with just one free throw. You step up to the line. Close your eyes. Your heart is palpitating. Your arm extends vertically. The ball is at your fingertips. You push it off. You miss the first shot. You bounce the ball in quiet anger. Your teammates, your coach, your fans, and your parents are waiting with crossed fingers and anticipation for the second shot. The arm is raised. The orange, round object flips off of your fingertips. You look out of one eye. The fans hear *swish!* Nothing but net! The fans are going crazy. You glance over at the coach, who is wiping off big drops of sweat while popping a low-dose aspirin. Your team is up by one point with two seconds on the clock, and the opposing team has no time-outs left. Just a quick inbound play, and your team is headed to the state championship game. You just pulled off the biggest free throw of your life.

This happens often in gyms across America. Could this happen at your gym soon? Teams win many games when players make a high percentage of their free throws.

All around the world, you will find every basketball player warming up before the game, shooting nothing but jumpers from every point on the court. Rarely do you see a player warming up at the free-throw line. At the end of the game, if you had to evaluate each player who took a shot, what would the percentages look like? Or would you leave the gym with your head down, complaining that your team stunk at the free-throw line, making less than 50 percent of their free throws? Why are teams leaving "free" points on the table?

To be the best shooter or high-percentage free-throw shooter in the country, it takes more than just practice. You must envision yourself shooting the perfect shot not only in practice but also in the games. A perfect shot is when the ball ignores the rim and hits nothing but net. I believe a basket made that hits the rim is equal to a missed shot. My theory is that when you are so accustomed to hitting nothing but net that during game day, if you are off a little, you will still make the shot. With that being said, I have a prescriptive plan to turn your bad habits and low-percentage shooting into high-percentage shooting in a very short time. Through the pages of this book, the Shot Doctor will unveil his secret to teaching his son to become the best shooter and the most efficient scorer in the country by hitting nothing but net.

Shot Doctor video: To see the Shot Doctor in action, watch this 3:44 video. http//:youtu.be/4YAN6zxJIGE

Table of Contents

The Shot Doctor's Golden Nuggets· · · · · · · · · · · · · · vii
Acknowledgments ·ix
Foreword ·xi
Preface· xiii
Chapter 1   The Agony of Defeat: Get back up again! · · · · · · · · · 1
Chapter 2   LICARDS: Leading by Example · · · · · · · · · · · · · · · 9
Chapter 3   To Be or Not to Be Parent and Coach · · · · · · · · · · · 17
Chapter 4   Life of a King · 23
Chapter 5   Making House Calls: Meet the Shot Doctor · · · · · · · 29
Chapter 6   Own It, Bring It, Get It! · · · · · · · · · · · · · · · · · · · 33
Chapter 7   Numbers Don't Lie · 37
Chapter 8   Art of Shooting · 41
About the Author · 53

1
The Agony of Defeat: Get back up again!

When I was a player on Conway High School team in Conway, Arkansas, shooting was my claim to high school fame. Yes, in the pages of the Wampus Cats' annals, you will find Leroy McClure Jr.'s name as a shooting guard/forward. I love to shoot. Everywhere I went as a teenager, I had a ball in my hand because I needed to have the feel of a basketball. I dreamed of playing college basketball.

During my senior year at Conway High School in 1978, our basketball team was number one in the state of Arkansas. I was one of the top guards/forwards in the state. As we entered into the state playoffs, Conway Wampus Cats were predicted to win it all. We were beating Forest City by thirty points at halftime, and I had scored twenty-eight points. I was in a zone, and no one could stop me. I was scoring all over the court before I twisted my ankle with one minute before halftime. It was a serious sprain that kept me from playing in the second half. Unfortunately, Forest City made a comeback in the second half and tied the game. The game went into overtime. We lost by one point. I sat helplessly, watching my team lose a thirty-point lead in sixteen minutes. What a horrible way to finish my senior year in high school. Even though I had several scholarship offers to play basketball, I was finished with basketball. I did not want to see a basketball. I took the blame for that loss, and I felt my whole life had fallen apart. I felt defeated after that lost. I was devastated. I did not want to see a basketball for the rest of my life. I reminded myself that "the godly may trip seven times, but they will get up again. But one disaster is enough to overthrow the wicked" (Proverbs 24:14). Somewhere deep in my heart, I knew that I would never give up on my dream. I had basketball in my veins.

When I graduated from high school, I moved to Dallas with a friend to pursue an education in engineering at a local proprietary school. I walked away from the game of basketball from March 1978 to April 1979.

Get Back Up Again

While attending an engineering school, I was missing the game of basketball. I could not take it anymore. I had to find a school with a basketball program. I visited Richland Community College, a community college in Dallas, to see if I could get back into playing basketball. I asked to talk to Coach Louis Stone, the men's head basketball coach of Richland, about trying out for the basketball team. Coach Stone asked me if I could play. I told him I could play but I had not played in a year. He found me some shoes, took me to where the team was scrimmaging, and put me in the game with the team. I immediately shot the ball. I realized that my shot had never left me. Coach Stone stood in amazement that no one could stop me from scoring, especially since I had not played for one year. Shooting was my forte. I was very rusty with my dribbling and my passing. I eventually made the team later on during tryouts.

As a result of making the team, my number one goal was to improve my shooting efficiency rate. I was blessed to play two years at Richland College and led the team to two conference championships. In addition, I was selected as the Most Valuable Player (MVP) during my last year, when I averaged twenty points, ten assists, and five steals.

After the two years at the junior college, I landed a scholarship to play basketball and finish my bachelor's degree at Mayville State

University in Mayville (MSU), North Dakota. I was thrilled to get to play on a new stage more than 1,100 miles from home. Where in the world was North Dakota? Mayville had frigid temperatures of forty below zero with twenty inches of snow on the ground, and the town's favorite pastime was ice fishing on the frozen lake. It was so cold that when you sprayed afro moisturizer on your hair and went outside, all of your hair fell out if you touched it. Despite the cold, I was on track to finish playing collegiate basketball and finish my college degree.

The MSU fans were excited for a set of recruits who would position them to win their conference. Before the excitement could even quiet down my first year, I sprained my ankle before the season started. Since it was a serious sprain, the coaches decided to redshirt me. Initially, I did not like this decision because I was a baller and all I wanted to do was shoot basketball. I was down again. This time, I believed I would not get up again. I was highly touted by the school and fans. Everyone expected me to make an instant impact. Unlike high school, I had a team of experts who had a workout plan, a team of trainers to assist with the rehabilitation, and an opportunity to keep my scholarship for the two years. I strongly believe that "all things God works for the good of those who love him, who have been called according to his purpose." (Romans 8:28). I kept replaying in my mind that "all means all."

Around Christmastime, a local semi-professional team named Mayville-Portland started their season. They recruited me to play with them even though it had only been ten weeks since I twisted my ankle. I could run up and down the court half speed, but I had no quickness. All they wanted me to do was shoot the ball. I understood my role very well. In fact, during most games, my ankle would bother me so much that for twenty minutes, I would put my foot into a bucket of ice to alleviate the pain. Immediately upon returning to the game, I scored all of my points from the three-point range even though there was not a three-point line during the early

1980s. Instead of averaging twenty-eight points per game, I would have been averaging forty points per game if the three-point shot was in place. My ankle was so weak and unreliable that I was afraid to drive to the basket, so I stayed out of the paint. I had no problem shooting the ball from long distance before someone guarded me. My shooting range was between twenty-three and twenty-eight feet out. At half time, I put my foot and ankle in a bucket of ice for fifteen minutes. Once again, at the end of the game, I had a repeat performance of twenty-eight points. At the end of the season, Mayville-Portland played in the largest semi-professional basketball tournament in North Dakota. This tournament was held in Minot, North Dakota, in March 1982.

I led the semi-professional team to win the State Class B Championship by averaging twenty-eight points per game in six games. My shots came from every point on the floor. I was in a zone, and I scored at will. Many fans came to the game to see me put on a shooting exhibition. They had heard about this African American with an afro who could shoot from anywhere on the court. Keep in mind that some of these fans had not seen African Americans in person, only on television. I carried myself like an ambassador for my people, especially on the court. In fact, I was named to the All-Tournament Team and the Most Valuable Player of the tournament.

The following season, I returned to play my final two years of eligibility on the Mayville State University basketball team, where I helped them win the conference title. As a non-starter, I averaged double figures. My main role on the team was a shooter. My shooting would spread out the defense. During one game, I was on a roll where I made three three-pointers in a row when a defender hit my shooting hand. Diagnosis: two dislocated fingers. The coach frantically called a timeout. I freaked out when I looked down and saw my fingers. They were dislocated, bending backward, almost touching my wrist. The trainers put them back in place and taped the two fingers together. I ran back to the court immediately, making two more three-pointers to lead our team to a win against Valley City. To accomplish this feat, I was applying the components of the art of shooting—**N**inety-degree angle (elbow), **B**ackspin, **A**rc, and **F**ollow-through.

EXCERPTS FROM AN ARTICLE
Mayville-Portland amateur cagers claim class B title
B-2 Trail County Tribune
March 31, 1982

Leroy McClure was selected to the five-member State B amateur basketball All-Tournament team after Mayville-Portland won the State Championship Sunday afternoon. McClure, a junior at Mayville State College, who was also named the tournament's Most Valuable Player, averaged twenty-eight points a game in the six games the May-Port team played. The team title was the first ever for the May-Port team as the amateurs downed four-time defending champion Watford City in the title game Sunday afternoon.

Mayville-Portland won six games in the North Dakota class B amateur basketball tournament held in Minot last weekend to claim the State Championship for the first time in the history of the team.

McClure was named to the class B all-tournament team, which was comprised of just five players.

McClure, who was named the tournament's Most Valuable Player while averaging twenty-eight points in the six games, was a member of the Mayville State basketball team this past winter but was redshirted and will have two years of eligibility remaining at Mayville.

Mayville-Portland opened play in the amateur tournament Thursday by clubbing Mohall 122–64. McClure got his scoring in rolling by netting thirty points:

In the amateurs' second game, Mayville-Portland downed Kulm 108–75 as McClure and Rygg again provided the 1–2 scoring punch with thirty-two and twenty-two points, respectively.

In their only game Friday, Mayville-Portland handled Center 110–81 as five players scored in double figures. McClure had his lowest-scoring performance of the tournament and settled for twenty-five points but still led Mayville-Portland scorers.

In the quarterfinal round Saturday, the Mayville-Portland amateurs stopped Beulah by a 109–97 score. McClure took a backseat in scoring for the first time but still poured through 26 tallies.

In the semifinal play Saturday night, Mayville-Portland stopped Havana 105–75 as six players scored in twin digits. McClure popped in twenty-eight to lead the way...

In the game for the state class B championship, Watford City fell to the Mayville-Portland scoring machine by a 111–93 score. McClure poured through thirty-five points to lead the way...

The ball finally went flat for me. I left MSU with a dashed dream of furthering my career of either playing European basketball or professional basketball. My shooting career had ended. *Here I am, Lord, "send me."* I returned to Dallas with my computer analyst degree in hand and my basketball in the trunk. I was down again! How can I get back up again? I kept Apostle Paul's words resonating in my mind: "Forgetting what is behind and straining toward what is ahead, I press on toward the goal to win the prize." (Philippians 3:13–15).

Chapter 1 Summary

1. Learn early to never walk away from a person or game you really love. Hang in there until the decision is no longer in your hand.
2. Whatever the circumstance was that made you consider walking away, allow that event to be a stepping-stone in turning an adversity into a victory.
3. Do not stay down as if you are defeated. Get back up again!
4. "Consider it pure joy my brothers, the various trials you may encounter. The testing of your faith produces endurance and endurance causes you to be more perfect and more complete, lacking nothing." James 1:2-4

2
LICARDS: Leading by Example

I landed a job at Texas Instruments as a computer analyst. I wadded up paper and shot it in my wastebasket as I went from cubicle to cubicle. I was bored. I was distracted. I was so unfocused. My undiagnosed attention deficit disorder was in high gear. I did very little work. You guessed it: I was finally discharged from this job. I felt lower than Jonah in the belly of a big fish. My brother, Sam, introduced me to education. He told me that he was teaching physical education to children with learning disabilities (LD). Even though these students were bright, they could not read because they were dyslexic or had attention deficit hyperactivity disorder (ADHD) or attention deficit disorder (ADD). Through Sam's work experience, he was diagnosed as dyslexic. We knew growing up that Sam's struggles with reading were more than just being lazy. Sam and I are thirteen months apart. I always had to do all of his work in high school. As he continued to describe the private-school students with learning disabilities, I felt as though I had strong characteristics of ADD. He convinced me to work with LD students. The light bulb went off. I must get focused.

I became a man on a mission. I received a vision from the Lord to start a non-profit organization called FOCUS Centre of Learning, Inc. The word FOCUS was an acronym for Focus On Children in United States. I was concerned about the high illiteracy and drop-out rates in the African American community, and my brother's dyslexia propelled me to complete a four-year certification to become the only African American male Certified Academic Language Therapist trained in the Orton-Gillingham teaching method designed to work with struggling readers. I was up again!

Although I was always focused on basketball, I had to concentrate on a new profession that would enable me to make a difference. As I worked with LD students with reading and physical education, I noticed that even though they may not have been the most skilled players, it was the pats on the back when they did good things in the classroom and on the basketball floor that propelled them to even greater heights and accomplishments. It was a light-bulb moment for me. As a teacher and athletic coach, I needed to continue to motivate those students. It was my responsibility to go far beyond giving pep talks. I set out to be a role model for excellence. I encouraged their growth by creating a positive environment. I built a rapport with those students/players. I began to point out their strengths and noted any improvement in their performance. I treated their mistakes as learning opportunities— I never punished them for their mistakes.

Coach McClure was growing in the teaching and coaching professions. I begin to believe sports do build and reveal character. I began instilling in my students seven-character qualities called LICARDS: leadership, integrity, character, accountability, responsibility, discipline, and self-esteem.

I trained young children to be disciplined as they learned to read and learned the art of shooting the ball. I was excited to see some of the student athletes become good students and players because they listened and followed through on what they learned. Oftentimes, LD students are characterized as misfits. Thanks in part to basketball and emphasizing the LICARDS, my students finally had a way to overcome their low self-esteem.

I drilled and drilled them by repeating the definitions of the seven character qualities. Basketball had a way of lifting the esteem of those students when they realized they could make free throws, consistently shoot the ball in the goal, and even score points to win a game. I saw the value of repeating letters and key words to students as they learned to read. I saw the value of shooting one hundred free throws a day to assist an athlete to win a game at the free-throw line. I saw students overcoming low self-esteem issues and rising to the place of leadership, responsibility, and accountability both in the classroom and on the basketball court. I was back in the game of life through the students believing in me and me believing in the students. The LICARDS' qualities refreshed me and propelled me to dream again. A new vision was birth. I could even hear the SWISH again.

In the early 1990s, I hired a law firm to write and file the paperwork for a 501(c)(3) status. I was on a mission with an eagerness to teach students with learning disabilities because of having observed first-hand the learning struggles of my brother Sam in school. I finally received a 501(c)(3) determination status letter for FOCUS. I was in pursuit of working with children, but I needed help.

Boy Meets Girl

I was focused! Ironically, when I contacted a marketing organization, it was named Focus Communication. I set up a meeting with this group at a restaurant. Upon my arrival to this lunch appointment, a gray car approached me. The window rolled down, and this young woman asked if I was Herman. Under my breath, I said, "I wish I was." I went into the restaurant awaiting my appointment. I happened to notice the young woman from the car was waiting, too. I asked her whom she was waiting for, and she said someone from Focus Communication. This organization was trying to hire her to be on their public relations/marketing team. Finally, each of our appointments from Focus showed up. We met individually with our appointments.

After an hour-long meeting, both groups departed. As we walked down the stairs, we stopped to talk further. The young woman told me to not believe anything that this group told me. I asked her about her occupation. She told me that her background was a degree in journalism and she had experience working in print, radio, and television media. At this time, she was working in her own public relations and marketing business. I gave her a business card. Three days later, I arranged a meeting with this young woman. Since our first meeting, we prayed together every day because I told her I was "focused," and this is why I named the company FOCUS.

This young woman wrote a grant for $20,000 to open up a facility to house a private learning center to teach LD students to read with private instruction at FOCUS Centre of Learning, Inc., in Richardson, Texas. I resigned from my job as teacher and coach to pursue the dream of helping struggling African American students learn to read. Nine months later, I proposed to my PR/Marketing and grant writer. We were married on March 16, 1996. Therefore, Mrs. Yvette McClure and I began to open our hearts, lives, and homes to many struggling readers.

I began to work with LD students within both private and public schools but soon realized that students in the South Dallas/Oak Cliff area face many social and economic barriers, experience staggering dropout and illiteracy rates, and lack the resources to get culturally appropriate help. I felt led to assist non-affluent students with learning challenges who might not otherwise receive the help. I began to dream of a center where comprehensive services for LD children could be provided from within the southern Dallas community.

Another grant opportunity came across our desk. My wife wrote a grant to not only go into two elementary schools to teach the students to read but to also to operate a multi-sensory basketball program focusing on character qualities using the seven LICARDS. The 75216 Initiative was a program sponsored by a Texas state senator specifically for students who lived in Dallas' zip code 75216 where the highest crime rate existed. The funding was for innovative educational, leadership, and sports programs.

This program was an instant hit for students. I also created a program to train teachers to teach children with learning differences. I started the FOCUS Teacher Training Program (FTTP) where more than fifty men and women have been trained in the Orton Gillingham alphabetic phonics program to work with children who struggle to read.

Our personal lives began to change, too. On September 30, 1996, my wife was admitted to Baylor Hospital, where she spent seventeen hours in labor and finally had a baby by Caesarean section at 2:35 a.m. on October 1, 1996. We had been studying the Bible character King David. We pitched the idea to name him King David or Joshua. My wife was on her knees in intensive labor to help the baby to turn correctly because he was face up and pushing incorrectly in the birth canal. We knew this impactful birth had to be meaningful and purposeful. When our son was born, he stood straight up whistling. He stood tall. With our time studying King David, the tender warrior who was after God's own heart, we decided to keep the name King, but add my dad's and my first name as his middle name. King's late grandfather is Leroy McClure Sr., and I am Leroy Jr. The newborn baby boy named King LeRoy McClure made an intensive and excruciating entry into the world.

Little did I know that teaching and coaching would lead me to start a school as a full-time business. In order to support my family, my wife continued to write grants to establish programs in the southern part of Dallas with emphasis on character, academics, and athletics. Another grant award landed me an opportunity to do an alphabetic phonics program at a private school. I juggled working for myself, supporting my stay-at-home wife, and playing pickup ball and even playing games on Saturday with an organized adult basketball team.

With the baby in arm, my wife continued hitting the keystrokes on the computer putting plans into motion for growing our reading and sports programs. A year later, I received an invitation to a meeting regarding charter schools. My wife encouraged me to attend the meeting. The charter school movement had just started in Texas in 1995. To apply, I had to write a proposal to the Texas Education Agency (TEA). In November 1997, I drove the charter application to Austin, but it had to be timed stamped by 5:00 p.m. I got lost and made it to the right floor five minutes after closing time. I missed the deadline. I was knocked down to the floor. I cried and prayed, but to no avail. The rejected proposal was mailed back to us.

We moved our business from the north side to the southern Dallas area to be closer to my consultant jobs. This time, my wife was seven months pregnant, very sickly, and trying to pack to move to our new home. Two months before the move, I received a notice that the third generation of charter schools would be accepting applications. She had fifteen-month-old King in the left arm and the right hand pecked away on the keyboard. We had to hurry to get this charter written and in Austin before the deadline of July 24, 1998.

Wouldn't you know it—my wife went into labor while writing the charter school application. She went into the hospital at 5:30 a.m. on July 22, 1998. She begged the doctors to allow her to bring her laptop to the hospital. They said no. We knew that the first delivery was laborious and figured this would be no different. To our surprise, my wife tried to deliver naturally, but again the baby was face up and headed away from the birth canal, crushing the baby's face and upper parts of the body. My wife was prepped for another Caesarean section. This time, we received a bit of a shocker. The doctors had to remove a thick layer of scar tissue from the top of my wife's stomach. She now required plastic surgery in the midst of an unfinished charter school application. I refused to believe I was being kicked down again. They finally delivered a healthy baby girl by Caesarean section at 7:30 p.m. on July 22. My wife looked at my happy face but could feel my silent disappointment with the unfinished document. She told me to go home, get the laptop, and she would finish the document. I ran out of Baylor Hospital as if I was running a 4.3 forty-yard dash. She finished that charter application the next day. I headed to a copy center for the required copies and to the overnight delivery service. The charter made it to Austin on time.

We received a confirmation and some changes within two months of submittal of the document. On the way to celebrate my wife's birthday on September 12, 1998, we received a call from the state's educational agency to inform us that the charter application was approved. FOCUS Learning Academy opened its doors on August 17, 1999, to one hundred K–6 students on the second floor at a southern Dallas church.

I used my private school experience and language science skills to help design the FOCUS education program and curriculum that both identifies and enrolls special needs students and teaches them to reach levels of recognized performance in reading and math. The vision of the FOCUS Learning Academy was to have a charter school that embodies a model program that has consistent high academics for generations to come and produces future leaders. This is a model that the country can and will adopt.

I finally had a focused-driven life. I was called Coach McClure, Coach, Mr. McClure, and now CEO/Superintendent McClure. I cherished those names and continued my pursuit of being a man on a mission.

Chapter 2 Summary

1. What do you want to be when you grow up?
2. What does our Heavenly Father wants you to be when you grow up?
3. Are they the same?
4. You must find your calling!
5. As you choose your career, make certain you are making an impact (change agent) to our society. Be relevant.

6. There is no better feeling to know that you are doing what you love and you are really good at it and you are getting paid to do it.
7. If the truth be told, you love what you do so much that you would do it for free.
8. "He who started a good work in you will be faithful to complete it." Philippians 1:6

3

To Be or Not to Be Parent and Coach

With the business growing, playing pickup basketball, and teaching Sunday school, I had to adjust my attitude quick, fast and in a hurry. Now, with two small children, I was not sure how to balance my time. I had a small fan cheering on the side, my little three-year-old son, King LeRoy McClure. He was dunking off of two feet in the kitchen chair on a rim hanging off the pantry door. I was not going to push my son to play basketball; it would have to be a natural progression.

Parent/Coach Relationship

At the age of four, I began to take King to the gym when I went to play with the adult league. He was dunking on his toy goals to imitate my moves. My wife encouraged me to take King to practices so that I could build a relationship with him. We knew that is was time to plant and water many seeds with King. We began to practice Deuteronomy 6:6–7: "These commandments that I give you today are to be on your hearts. Impress them on your children. Talk about them when you sit at home and when you walk along the road, when you lie down and when you get up." Like the students in the classrooms, it was time for me to exercise a full-court press with imparting a character-education plan to King.

King became increasingly keen in the game of basketball by the time he was five years old. He had big hands and was nicknamed "Bear Paws." He had a knack for moving the ball in a way that reignited a hot red-orange flame in my heart for the game of basketball. By age six, I began to coach him in basketball through a neighborhood recreation center. It was my time to build a relationship with my son, and basketball was the catalyst to the strong relationship that we have today. I noticed that the referees were allowing the kindergarten players to pick up the ball and walk with it down the floor. Oh no! I immediately went to the store and bought some orange cones. I sat them up in front of our house and began to teach King to dribble the basketball. He struggled at first because it was much work. When he got in the game and scored all twenty-two points by himself, it was the beginning of a basketball bond between father and son. From this moment, I was known as "Dribbling Daddy." I wanted to coach my son. It was fun. It seemed easy.

Research oftentimes says coaching your own son leads to conflicts at the gym and at home. For instance, the parent-coach and the son continue to argue at the dinner table about not performing well at a competition, or the son is frustrated with the parent's coaching tactics and does not want to talk to him or her for hours. I was determined not to fall victim to the negative talk about parents as coaches. I continued to build a strong basketball program with my son and other kids.

I joined a basketball organization where I was still able to coach my son and many young men and young women athletes from the 2015 high school graduating class who now have received scholarships to some of the top Division 1 basketball programs in the country. I worked my son out extremely hard after work and on Saturdays. We even won an international championship with an organization called Biddy Basketball.

My parenting style became more like Coach McClure than Daddy did. The father-son relationship slipped somewhat. As a father, there is nothing better than having a great relationship with your children—a relationship where you can accept them for who they are because "they are wonderfully and marvelously made," including warps, pimples and idiosyncrasies, and more. As my extreme coaching of not sitting down and instructing while in the game intensified, I had to remind myself that the unconditional love the Lord Jesus Christ has for me must be exhibited to my son and others. This love is known as agape love, a sacrificial love that is not based on feelings. It is an act of will to put other's welfare above my own.

I moved away from Biddy Basketball with a small ball to a major youth league called AAU (Amateur Athletic Union). This stage opened the door for me to launch Triple A Stallions. The Triple A represents attitude, academics, and athletics, in that order. It was clear to me that I must continue to nurture and cultivate a relationship with my son and the other players on the team. We made a great run under AAU's Triple A Stallions by placing fifth in the National AAU 10U tournament when King was in the fifth grade, but the father-son relationship was suffering. We begin to have some unforeseen issues such as some of the parents perceiving that I was only coaching so my son could be the best in the class and thinking that I was giving him preferential treatment.

It was hard to separate the coach from the dad. We had a rule at the house—when you turn into the driveway, you have to stop talking about basketball. My goal was to be the best father I could be for my son, not the best coach. I stopped coaching King at the end of fifth grade because my expectations for him were unrealistic. As a disciplinarian, I was strict—and still am strict, to a certain degree. I made the mistake of holding King to a higher level of accountability than his teammates. It is imperative for me to not get this relationship twisted because if I had not handled this delicate relationship the proper way with prayer, I could have lost my son. I cannot emphasize enough the power of prayers to discern when would be the right time to stop coaching my son, King. I needed to spend quality time and quantity time to get to know my son off the court, too. I found it to be okay to allow my son to speak his mind as long as he did it in a respectful way. In this manner, I was giving him a voice by listening to him instead of lecturing him. Because of this, he wanted to be in my presence most of the time. I used this time to impart knowledge, instruction, wisdom, and basketball since it was always on his mind. I feel very grateful that I have an opportunity to be a great dad just like my dad was to me. Of course, all relationships must be worked on, and my relationship with my son is no different.

Sports is an activity that we both share, and it gives us the greatest pleasure to build a bond that cannot be easily broken. When we watch football games or basketball games together, this leads us into interesting conversations that not only help us to get to know each other better but also help us to embrace the speed of trust. King knows he can always count on me and I will be there for him. Through conversations and deeds, I affirm King on a daily basis. Our conversations sometimes start with basketball, other sports, friends, church, scripture reading, abstinence, celebrities, and academics. However, it always ends with topics I feel are most important for his development emotionally and spiritually at that time.

As a parent and coach, I learned that you must be reflective. Your child is a human being, and you are a human being, too. Both of you possess emotions. You have to help your child see the big picture of staying involved within the sport for years to come. This requires hard work, commitment, and determination beyond where a child is as a youth player. My wife and I understood that while you are coaching, you have to be a coach, and when you are at home, you have to be a parent. Here is some advice to parents who coach their own child.

1. Give your child more praise and technical instruction based on his or her true abilities.
2. Relate basketball strategies to real-life strategies as often as you can.

3. Talk about the importance of character qualities on and off the court.
4. When you are home, be a parent.
5. Provide unconditional love and support. Do not bring home things that happened in practices and competitions.
6. Refrain from turning the dinner-table conversation to coaching criticism.
7. Talk about things other than sports with your child.
8. Tell your child that the rewards for learning to walk with the parent while he or she is in the day-to-day struggle with him or her will help prepare him or her for the real world of work and/or playing sports in college or professionally when he or she becomes an adult.

While on the journey of parenting and coaching, I discovered that your attitude and your approach to game day or home experiences shapes your child's altitude as a student, an employee, and a contributing or non-contributing citizen.

Chapter 3 Summary

1. Whatever you do, remember that charity (love in action) starts at home first.
2. Sharing a common interest with your child or children is like a slice of heaven when it leads to an unbreakable bond.
3. There is no better title I desire than being a parent. Not only do I see myself but I can make necessary adjustments so that my son can be a better version of me.
4. Dads must find out what their child's gift or talent is and help foster it with time and resources and not allow their own desire to overshadow the child's dream.
5. My goal is to be the best dad and not the best coach for my son.

6. When the two of us were in conflict, I resigned as a coach for my son. Because of this decision, I am a proud dad first.
7. "Parents do not provoke your children; instead, bring them up in the training and instruction of the Lord." Ephesians 6:4

4
Life of a King

New School Fit for a King and Princess

Triple A Academy is an open-enrollment public charter high school located in southwest Dallas. Our high school is the sister school to FOCUS Learning Academy. Triple A was envisioned in 1996 during the time when King LeRoy McClure was born. Yvette and I knew one day we would like to have a school that was excellent and good enough for our own children, even if it was not a Christian school. As a man of faith, we knew that our moral values are taught at home. While we would not teach the Bible at a public charter school, the scriptures are in us, and our moral values would be lived out wherever we go.

When I stopped coaching King and some other great players in the class of 2015 who were on Triple A Stallions AAU team. It was my dream to have a high school program that offered character-education programs, strong academics and outstanding athletics for our AAU players to attend. When King was in the seventh grade, our board of directors voted to expand our school to high school since our grade level only went up to the eighth grade. Then, we were able to gain Texas Education Agency's approval to add ninth through twelfth grades and rename the seventh- through twelfth-grade cluster Triple A Academy.

Our first year of high school only consisted of the ninth grade. It was during this time that we enrolled King in the eighth grade and

Princess in the seventh grade at Triple A Academy. Once King was enrolled, most of his basketball friends wanted to enroll, especially those on his summer basketball team. King's basketball friends from all over the Dallas–Fort Worth area applied for admission to Triple A Academy because they could really play basketball. However, they had discipline problems or academic issues, and they were not admitted to the school. Let us not forget what Triple A stands for: attitude, academics, and athletics. By law, charter schools do not have to admit students who have documented discipline cases. Contrary to popular opinion, Triple A is not a basketball school. Character development and academics comes first. At Triple A, our best players make the top scores on the state's high-stakes tests, have the highest grade point averages, and have impeccable character.

Your Attitude Determines Your Altitude

Out of all the conversations that King and I have had in the past, there is one that still resonates with me. King shared with me that he wanted to be the best guard in the country. He asked me to help him. Let me say this again - he asked me, his father, to help him. Not only did I feel respected, but I felt honored that he saw the character traits in me along with the expertise to make his request a reality. He knew once I had given him my word, everything else was secondary; therefore, I started with what I do best. I can shoot the basketball. I am a shooter. Even at the age of fifty-plus, I can still shoot the ball. King has witnessed this many times since the age of three. I committed to teach him all that I knew so that someday he would be able to outshoot me. It was time for King to go to the lab.

For King to be the player or student athlete he is today, the foundation had to be in place first. I spent more time on attitude since this is the quality that sidelines most athletes, businesspeople, and leaders. I fundamentally believe that your attitude determines your altitude. I sat out to be the best dad and coach with my son. We have adopted this model in our home that good coaches win games, but great coaches change lives. I started with a lifetime change by emphasizing character qualities that would last King for a lifetime.

Discipline

I know from personal experience that accurate and efficient shooting requires great discipline. Here is the problem. People oftentimes believe that discipline is negative—a way to punish someone to ensure that rules or orders are obeyed. I tend to believe being disciplined is to train yourself to do something by controlling your behavior. I developed a training regimen for King at an early age because you must be disciplined in order to be the best guard in the country. King had to adapt to discipline as a norm far greater than most kids did in their formative years.

The basketball is like his best friend. He has worn out over a dozen of basketballs because of his love for the game. I constantly remind him, "Whatever you do, do it with enthusiasm, and do it as if you are doing it for the Lord and not for man." (Colossians 3:23) I have watched King continue to get better in the game of basketball because many times, I am out there training and teaching him in the basketball lab. When he gets in the game, the preparation has already been done. During the game, he may only need a few mental reminders to rise above some momentary nuisances such as someone grabbing his shirt trying to harass him to take him out of his game. King simply has to remember if they foul him, he will be at the free-throw line confident in making it count.

Reality check! If you have not trained an athlete to shoot the ball with accuracy and efficiency, do not expect him or her to be successful. Remember, nothing from nothing leaves nothing. It works the same way in reading. If I have not taught my students the letters of the alphabet and the sounds associated with each letter, I cannot expect them to be an efficient reader. You can expect anything, but you can only inspect what you have taught.

Abilities, Preparation, Execution

A formula for an athlete's high performance is based on his or her ability, preparation, and then execution. All players have varying degrees of ability. A coach must realistically assess an athlete's ability, whether it is someone else's or your own child. Once you assess your athlete's abilities, you should develop a plan to aide in his or her preparation. This works the same in education. A teacher must know his or her students and then develop a lesson plan to ensure that he or she is meeting the needs of every learner. The preparation leads to the execution to ensure the student achieves the desired results at the end of a unit and/or the state's required test.

In the basketball world, the preparation is likened to an Olympian versus a recreational player or an A student versus a C student. The Olympian or the A student works on his or her weak skills while the recreational player or the C students works on his or her strengths or what he or she already knows. To be the best shooter or student requires understanding your abilities, being prepared in the offseason or days before the test, and being ready to execute in the real game or at the state's test. Even though you may lay the best plan out, you will still have to make the adjustments. A kid will still be a kid. In fact, King went from the eighth grade to the eleventh grade without a cell phone. The phone was a major distraction. We had to put other rules in place to keep him focused. For example, he played video games and watched television only on weekends. Insanity is doing the same thing over and over, expecting to get a different result.

Prescriptive Plan of Attack

A committed athlete knows it takes over ten thousand hours of a certain discipline to become a top collegiate or professional player. King's goal was to surpass these ten thousand hours. Why? Because he wants to be the best guard in the country.

While King has great work ethics, they did not happen overnight. Those work ethics were developed over time and at the right age of maturation. His workout routine may vary, depending on whether it is during the basketball off-season or regular season. Here is King's plan of attack:

- Shoot five hundred to six hundred shots, focusing on nothing but net three to four times per week
- Shoot one hundred free throws, focusing on nothing but net three to four days per week
- Do one hundred push-ups per day
- Swim three days per week at 7:30 a.m. during the summertime or do a water workout in a pool at a fitness club
- Work four days a week with an athletic trainer, focusing on building the core (stomach area and back), muscles supporting knees, and ankles.
- Eat the right food, staying away from things like starches and sugars, as well as drinking one hundred ounces of water every day.

Chapter 4 Summary

1. My goal was to create a school that is not only good for the public, but also good enough for my own children.
2. Character development is knitted into the fabric of our school culture. I have a hands on approach. One day I might give you some dap and the next day you might need a tap (corporal discipline).
3. To be the best (guard), ten thousands of hours are required. You are in the gym when your friends are at the movies. Your friends are with their girlfriends when the basketball is your girlfriend.

4. Laziness pays off now, but hard work pays off in the future.
5. Do you have a prescriptive plan to be the best or do you think by faith it will all work out?
6. Remember, "faith without works is dead." James 2:20
7. "Raise up a child the way they should go, and when they're old they will not turn from it." Proverbs 22:6

5

Making House Calls: Meet the Shot Doctor

Making House Calls

When you have the throbbing, constant pain of a headache, you go to see a neurologist. When you have stomach pain, you go the internal medicine doctor. When your eyes are hurting, you go to an ophthalmologist. When you are the main shooter on your basketball team shooting twenty-seven shots and only making twelve shots per game, what specialist do you visit?

From King's scoring all of his team's twenty-two points as a five-year-old to win a recreational league game to now averaging thirty-two points a game as a high school senior, can be attributed to a specialist – me, the Shot Doctor. I made a house call starting in my own house with my son. It started with a prescriptive plan.

While developing incredibly talented athletes, you have to keep them grounded with sayings like "when much is given much is required," "if better is out there, then good is not good enough," and "laziness pays off now, but hard work pays off in the future." Even when King was a small child, we had to impose tighter controls and higher levels of discipline and accountability for the results to pan out when he would be in a position to compete for athletic scholarships to top universities as a senior.

My advice to my own son started with my dad. I was reminded of my dad when I walked through the McClure Athletic Complex, which is named for my dad, Leroy McClure Sr. On the plaque that bears his picture and name, it reads, "No man stands tall until he stoops down to help a child." I followed his advice by building a facility more than thirty thousand square feet to extend our educational program. The facility has showcased the talents of kindergarten through fourth graders who play on the FOCUS Fun League basketball team, many rising athletes, and current and past professional basketball players.

I focus my eyes upon the banner bearing the state championship title for Conference 1A won by Triple A Academy Boys Varsity Basketball team in 2013. Our school was the first and only charter school to win a state championship under the University Interscholastic League (UIL). My reflection was short-lived as one of the coaches I admire very much approached me. He said that he now knows what to call me. "Instead of Mr. McClure, I will now call you the Shot Doctor," he said with a serious look on his face.

Hearing this was not a surprise. This was confirmation that my technique of teaching shooting had really been paying off not only with my son but also with his teammates. One of our players had been struggling with his shot. I took him back to the fundamentals of shooting by reviving his shot with correct rotation (backspin) on his shot. As a result, he is shooting a very high percentage from the field. Now that I have had major success with King's shooting efficiency and helping his teammate, I decided to let you in on the secrets to the "art of shooting" from the Shot Doctor. Remember, shooting is all about mechanics and repetition. I am responsible for the mechanics, and you are responsible for the repetition. To be a great shooter, it will take at least ten thousand hours of perfect practice where you are focusing on hitting nothing but net. If you do not consistently practice the mechanics I teach you, you will not be a successful shooter.

Chapter 5 Summary

1. When much is given, much is required.
2. Insanity is when you keep doing the same thing expecting to get different result.
3. Wisdom is when you call the Shot Doctor because your shot is off and you needs some help.
4. I can teach you the mechanics of shooting but you are responsible for the repetition.
5. To be one of the best shooters, it will take over ten thousand hours of perfect practice in shooting.
6. "The student is not above their teacher. It is enough for a student to be like their teacher." Matthew 10:24

6
Own It, Bring It, Get It!

Do It with Energy

There is a saying that is worth repeating: "Whatever you do, do it with enthusiasm as if you are doing it for the Lord." Nothing great happens unless there is some positive energy being expressed. If you were taking out the trash, do it with positive energy. If you are cleaning your room, do it with positive energy. If you are shooting a basketball, do it with positive energy. This type of energy is contagious, and it spreads like wildfire. I have seen the momentum of many basketball games shift behind the energy of one player. This player starts out by hustling, defending, and rebounding. While hustling, sometimes the player is diving on the floor for the ball. While playing defense, the player is getting steals and positioning his or her body to take a charge. When rebounding, the player is blocking out his or her man and getting offensive and defensive rebounds. The player has the attitude that he or she cannot be denied and is unstoppable with meeting the goal. This level of energy can psychologically take a team out of their game. When high energy is sustained, it can be the fuel that sparks the win.

In The Zone

In the zone (informal): In a state of focused attention or energy so that one's performance is enhanced.

Every good basketball player's desire should be to get "in the zone." The ultimate goal of a shooter is to get in the zone. A person would never understand what getting into a zone actually means unless you have been in it. Fortunately, I have been in a zone on the basketball court, and it is unlike any other experience while playing on the court. This experience is almost ineffable, but I will take my best shot at defining and explaining this experience with words. Being "in the zone" is when you are shooting a basketball in a game and you cannot miss. No matter how difficult or far away the shot is, you make it look really easy. When you can get the ball up, it will go in. It is almost like shooting the ball up in the clouds, and then our Lord just takes the ball, grabs it, and puts it in the basket for you. The higher you shoot it, the more net you will hit. The more shots you take, the more baskets you make. It is almost as if you cannot miss a shot, no matter where you shoot it from.

Lately, I have witnessed a few times when my son, King, was "in the zone." He did not miss a shot. Let me ask you this question. Who do you know on any level that has scored fifty points or more and took less than twenty-three shot attempts? King not only did it once, but he did it twice.

The first time for the fifty-point high was in a championship game in a high school tournament in Austin. He was nineteen out of twenty-three from the field, seven out of nine with three-pointers, twelve out of fourteen with two-pointers, and five out of six free throws. King had eighteen points in the first quarter, twelve points in the second quarter, ten points in the third quarter, and ten points in the fourth quarter. What makes this game so interesting is that King was really sick at halftime. He came over to me and said he was sick and needed to vomit. I showed him a trash can to use. I told him that he must go back in the game for the second half because this game could still go either way. He tried to convince me that I did not understand how he felt. I did not give in. Finally, I said "King, go to the top of the key, and shoot a three-point shot. If you make it, you play, and if you miss it, you can sit down the second half." King went to the top of the key and haphazardly threw the ball up, trying to miss the shot. He hit nothing but net—the perfect shot. Yes, I knew he was weak and sick, but he could still shoot because he was in the zone. The second half was no different because King only missed three shots and scored twenty points while feeling sick. He was the difference in the second half and put the game away with his "nothing but net" jumpers. Despite being sick, it was being in the zone that propelled King to score fifty points to lead his team to victory over the number one team in the state in 4A team.

The second time I saw King in the zone was at his school's home gym, McClure Athletic Complex against a rival 4A district team. The game was fast-paced. King's team put on a full-court press and started the game with a 15–0 lead. King had several steals and crowd-pleasing dunks.

The opposing team hung in there and did not quit. At halftime, King's team was only up by seven points. King exploded in the third quarter. He made six straight three-pointers and scored twenty points in the third quarter. He was in a zone. He blew the game open with his play and finished the quarter with a tomahawk dunk. When King left the game with six minutes left in the fourth quarter, the score was 89–51. King had fifty-one points. He had seventeen out of twenty field goals, six out of eight three-pointers, eleven out of twelve two-pointers, and eleven out of thirteen free throws.

In order for you to get in the zone, you must practice or understand the importance of shooting a perfect shot—nothing but net. Remember, the zone begins with what you do in the off-season preparation and routines.

Chapter 6 Summary

1. Whatever you do, do it with energy!
2. All of the great things that has happened in life, happened with energy and enthusiasm.
3. Being "in the zone" is when you are shooting a basketball in a game and you can't miss a shot.
4. In order to get in a zone, you must understand the importance of shooting a perfect shot and this begins with how you practice shooting in the off-season.
5. Every good basketball player's desire is to get "in the zone".
6. "Do you not know in a race all runners run, but only one will get the prize. Run in a way for you to receive the prize." 1 Corinthians 9:24-25

7

Numbers Don't Lie

Math Really Counts

Numbers are universal throughout the world. We can always hold ourselves accountable because numbers never lie. What does math have to do with shooting a basketball? Always keep the end in mind. Your success in shooting a basketball is measured by your shooting percentage made with your free throws, two-point field goals, and three-point field goals.

The art of shooting is based on a data-driven model. If you are shooting 100 percent from the free-throw line, you do not need my help. If you are shooting 100 percent from the two-point field goal, you do not need my help. If you are shooting 100 percent from the three-point line, you do not need my help. Do the math. If you are not shooting 100 percent, you need my help.

What is a good percentage to aim for free throws?

Type of Shot	Practice	Game
Free throws	95 percent	88 percent
Two-pointers	90 percent	75 percent
Three-pointers	80 percent	60 percent

The goal should be 95 percent in practice and 88 percent in the game. Let the Shot Doctor check your free-throw pulse.

Free throws are free. There is no reason why you should not make 95 percent of free throws. Many people would tell you that you need to practice shooting free throws. I tell you something different. I believe you need to practice shooting thousands of perfect free throws. The art of shooting consists of hitting nothing but net. In the game, your free-throw percentage will equate to 88 percent because of different game scenarios from being tired to rushing a shot.

What is a good percentage to aim for with two-point field goals? The goal should be 90 percent in practice and 75 percent in the game. Let the Shot Doctor check your lungs. I believe you must make 90 percent of the two-point shots after shooting thousands of perfect two-point shots in practice. The goal for made shots must be nothing but net. This 90 percent will translate to 75 percent in game-time situation.

What is a good percentage to aim for three-point field goals? The goal should be 80 percent in practice and 60 percent in the game. Let the Shot Doctor check your heart rate. While practice shooting thousands of perfect three-point field goals, you should make 80 percent of your shots. But during a game situation, this percentage should translate to 60 percent.

Results

According to Max Preps, King McClure is not only in the top twenty-five scorers in high school, averaging 32.5 points per game, but he is also the most efficient shooter in the country. What is efficiency? King is the only player in the country with 2.0 points per shot (2.0 pps). Most players have 1.0 to 1.5 pps, and the elite scorers have 1.5 to 1.8 pps. He averaged two points for every shot he attempted. During the 2015 season, King averaged thirty-two points per game from sixteen shot attempts per game. This only happened because of a high FG%, of 65 percent, a high 2FG% of 76 percent, high 3FG% of 49 percent, a high FT% of 86 percent. King has always been a scorer, but it was not until he was sidelined with a dislocated patella (kneecap). This was when he envisioned himself as being the best guard in the country. During his recovery, he envisioned his setback for a major comeback to be the best shooter in the country. King followed the components of the art of shooting daily. He knew that laziness paid off now but that hard work paid off in the future. Becoming the best shooter in the country was not an accident for King. It was strategically planned after King asked me to help him be the best guard in the country. As his father, I took off the father's hat and became the Shot Doctor.

If you are not shooting over 86 percent from the free-throw line, if you are not shooting 76 percent from the two-point field goal, if you are not shooting 65 percent for all field goals, and if you are not shooting over 49 percent from the three-point line, who are you going to call? The Shot Doctor.

Chapter 7 Summary

1. Are you shooting 86% from the free throw line, 76% from the 2-point line, 49% from the 3-point line, and 65% for all field goals?
2. Are you often called a ball hog or a gunner?
3. Do you shoot more than 20 shots per game and not average 40 points per game?
4. Have you ever made 91 free throws in a row?
5. Numbers don't lie!
6. "I am going to make you fruitful and increase your numbers." Genesis 48:4

8
Art of Shooting

Nothing but net: An expression that means the shot swished through the basket without touching the rim.

Many times, you hear coaches and even parents telling the athlete, "Shoot the ball." The athlete looks up at the crowd, the coach, and the clock and then fires off a shot. Nine times out of ten, the athlete or the coach do not evaluate why the athlete missed the shot. Usually, an athlete will rush a shot, miss a shot, pass up on a good shot, make a poor shot selection, have poor form, be tired, or just not know how to shoot. Countless statistics often show that the leading scorer on the team shot less than 50 percent in the game. No matter what set of numbers you present, 1 out 5, 6 out of 17, or 15 out of 31, the percentage is still less than 50%. Why are athletes shooting with 35 percent or less accuracy and efficiency? The Shot Doctor can help you improve your shooting efficiency with his nothing but net shooting method.

Perfect Shot

As a basketball player, there are key words you must know and understand if it is your desire to be an efficient shooter.

Perfect shot—the same as nothing but net.

If you shoot a basketball and make the shot, three things could happen.

1. The ball hits the rim and goes in.
2. The ball hits the backboard and goes in.
3. The ball goes in and hits nothing but net.

Why is the perfect shot the same as nothing but net? Did you know that two basketballs can almost go into the goal at the same time? The diameter of an official NBA basketball hoop is eighteen inches, about an inch less than twice the diameter of a men's ball, which is 9.39 inches. Therefore, making a shot that hits the rim could be way off the mark but still go in. The perfect shot that hits nothing but net should be the desired result of every shot attempt. You should never settle for anything less when you are practicing the art of shooting.

The first rule of becoming an accurate and efficient shooter is understanding the math. This is only 50 percent of the equation. The other 50 percent is to understand the mechanics.

NBA-Follow-Through

The Shot Doctor has a formula to help you become an efficient shooter. The four components are as follows:

1. **N**-Ninety-degree angle (elbow): The elbow should be at a ninety-degree angle and slightly off to the right side so the shooter can see the basket and the ball.
2. **B**-Backspin: The rotation of the ball is essential. If you shoot the ball without backspin, the ball will probably bounce back to you. The backspin causes the net to swish and the ball to softly roll in if it hits the rim.
3. **A**-Arc: This refers to the arc on your shot. The higher the shot, the bigger the rim is when it finally lands. This is referred to as trajectory of the ball. The higher the arc, the bigger the target.

4. **F**-Follow-through: The ball must roll off of your fingertips. The shooting hand should extend through the basket. It should look like you are putting your hand in the basket.

Art of Shooting Summary

Let us review the NBA Follow-through component.

Ninety-degree angle (elbow) ▶ **B**ackspin, rotation ▶ **A**rc—get it up high ▶ **F**ollow-through—fingertip

Shooting Mechanics

To improve shooting efficiency, the Shot Doctor will analyze the mechanics of shooting free throws, two-point field goals and three-point field goals.

Preparations for Shooting

First, we start shooting at the backboard in the paint while adjacent to the goal on the left side. We start shooting the basketball up toward the backboard only using the four components of the art of shooting. I am watching for NBA Follow-through, which is 1. **N**inety-degree angle (elbow), 2.**B**ackspin, 3. **A**rc, and 4. **F**ollow-through. While my players are shooting approximately fifty shots, I will tell him or her which component is missing after each shot. You might hear me say, "Get it up, get it up; more rotation, more rotation; elbow straight, fingertip." Second, we repeat this routine on the right side of the goal. We put up fifty more shots while I am monitoring every shot and making comments on one of the four components when necessary. Thirdly, we get in front of the goal underneath it and focus on making the basket using backboard only. Again, focusing on **N**inety-degree angle (elbow), **B**ackspin, **A**rc, and **F**ollow-through. At this point, we have put up 150 shots, and now we are ready to move about eight feet out in the paint in front of the goal. Now our objective is to hit nothing but net. I will make a comment on every shot if it is not nothing but net. Getting it high and rotation are usually what are missing if the shot is not nothing but net. The goal is to make nothing but net on every shot. Once you get the feel of shooting nothing but net, then you move further back to eleven to twelve feet. You shoot another twenty-five or thirty shots, making certain that you are using all components of the art of shooting. You must make more perfect shots then and not before you move to the free-throw line.

Free throws

In the forty-five years in which I have played or coached basketball, there is one thing that I have found to be true. All good free-throw shooters are good jump shooters, but not all good jump shooters are good free-throw shooters. Using this as my compass, I feel compelled to always start teaching the art of shooting at the free-throw line. The free-throw line is always fifteen feet from the goal, and we have this distance always programmed in our minds. I have trained King to focus on shooting perfect free throws over the years by using the art of shooting technique. By using this technique, he once made ninety-one consecutive free throws. He shot 86 percent from the line during his senior year in high school. He made 212 out of 247 free throws.

This is how I do it. I initially get my player to shoot ten free throws and then rest. I get the player to shoot ten more free throws and rest. While shooting, I evaluate the shot, and I count the number of shots made. After doing this quick evaluation, I now have a benchmark for the free throws.

Shooting Free Throws

1. Shooting stance—your feet should be shoulder-width apart, and if you are right handed, your right foot should be three to four inches ahead of the other foot. If you are left handed, your left foot should be three to four inches ahead of your right foot.
2. Your knees must be slightly bended.
3. Dribble the ball one to three times. (Be consistent with the number of dribbles.)
4. You must apply all components of the art of shooting.
5. Your goal is to hit nothing but net, the perfect shot.
6. This is done ten times. After ten shots, you should apply the PDSA.
7. PDSA: Plan Do Study Adjust
8. Make adjustments to your shot depending on which components of the art of shooting are missing.
9. If the ball goes to the left or the right, straighten up your elbow. If the ball is long, look at front of the rim when shooting. If the ball is short, get the ball up high with more rotation when shooting.
10. Shoot one hundred free throws while applying #6, #7 and #8.
11. Your goal is to hit at least ten consecutive shots—nothing but net—while getting the feel of shooting the perfect shot at the same time. After shooting thousands of free throws, you should be able to make ninety-three to ninety-five free throws out of one hundred.

Two-Point Jump Shot

Two-point shots are taken more often than any other shot in a game. Unfortunately, the mid-range shot is a lost art. Everyone wants to shoot the three-point shot or they want to take the ball all the way to the hoop. No one wants to master the mid-range shot. I like to teach the mid-range shot from the elbow. This is where the free-throw line intersects the lane line on the left and right side. Most basketball gurus say that making over 50 percent of two-point field goal is good. I agree. However, what about being great? I believe a player should make 75 percent of his or her 2-point field goals. After twenty-seven games, King has made 201 out of 266 two-point field goals—76 percent. This is great! He takes almost ten two-point shots per game, and he makes 7.5 shots. A jump shot or a jumper is an attempt to score a basket by jumping straight up and in midjump, propelling the ball in an arc into the basket. A jump shot can be taken from the pass or off the dribble. I will talk about shooting from the pass first. The jumper from the pass can be very simple or more difficult, depending on accuracy of the pass. For simplicity purpose, we will assume all passes are accurate passes.

Two-Point off the Pass

The following steps should be taken to master the perfect jump shot off the pass:

1. Get squared up, facing the basket before receiving the ball.
2. Have knees slightly bent in a crouched position before receiving the ball.
3. Once you have received the ball, immediately get the ball in shooting position while jumping straight up into your midjump, propelling the ball in an arc into the basket.
4. Now, implement all components of the art of shooting.
5. For starters, shoot one hundred to two hundred shots three times a week. Advanced shooters, shoot four hundred to five hundred shots three times a week.
6. Remember, your goal is to shoot the perfect shot—nothing but net.

7. If it is not nothing but net, apply the components of the art of shooting that are lacking.
8. Remember, NBA Follow-through: 1. **N**inety-degree angle (elbow), 2. **B**ackspin, 3. **A**rc, 4. **F**ollow-through.

Two-Point off the Dribble

The following steps must be taken to master the perfect jump shot off the dribble.

1. Always dribble the basketball in a crouched position.
2. Square up, facing the basket while picking up the dribble.
3. Get the ball in shooting position while jumping straight up into your midjump, propelling the ball in an arc into the basket.
4. Now implement all components of the art of shooting.
5. For starters, shoot one hundred to two hundred shots three times a week. Advanced players, shoot five hundred to six hundred shots three times a week.
6. Remember, your goal is to shoot the perfect shot—nothing but net.
7. If it is not nothing but net, apply the components of the art of shooting that are lacking.
8. Remember, NBA Follow-through: 1. **N**inety-degree angle (elbow), 2. **B**ackspin, 3. **A**rc, 4. **F**ollow-through.

Three-Point Jump Shot

There are two plays in the game of basketball that can change the momentum of a game. They are a slam dunk and a three-point shot. These made baskets are called game changers. I would like to focus on the three-point shot. This shot is probably the most difficult shot to make on the basketball court because it is the farthest away from the basket—at least twenty feet away. However, I believe a player can shoot 50 percent from the three-point line if they are properly trained and properly coached. Yes, I know the basketball gurus report that 35 percent is a good number. I wholeheartedly disagree. Maybe this is true in college or the NBA because I have not been there yet. However, in high school, I have my son shooting right at 49 percent, and he takes only sixteen shots a game while 6.5 of them are three-pointers. According to Max Preps, 84–172, King's three-point FG% is the highest of the top twenty-five scorers in the country when the average three-point field goal percentage from this elite group is 36 percent. So, Mr. Shot Doctor, what are you saying? Do not believe this 35 percent garbage for three-point field goal percentage accuracy. Visualize making half of your shots from the three-point line. Can you see it? I can see 50 percent also. Now let us get to work.

Start practicing shooting your three-point shot from the top of the key because it is much easier to make three-pointers from the top of the key than from the wings or the corners.

Three-Point off the Pass

The following steps should be taken to master the perfect jump shot off the pass.

1. Get squared up, facing the basket before receiving the ball.
2. Have your knees slightly bent in a crouched position before receiving the ball.
3. Once you have received the ball, immediately get the ball in shooting position while jumping straight up into your midjump, propelling the ball in an arc into the basket.
4. Now implement all components of the art of shooting.
5. For starters, shoot one hundred to two hundred shots three times a week. Advanced shooters, shoot four hundred to five hundred shots three times a week.

6. Remember, your goal is to shoot the perfect shot—nothing but net.
7. If it is not nothing but net, apply the components of the art of shooting that are lacking.
8. Remember, NBA Follow-through: 1. **N**inety-degree angle (elbow), 2. **B**ackspin, 3. **A**rc, 4. **F**ollow-through.

Three-Point off the Dribble

The following steps must be taken to master the perfect jump shot off the dribble.

1. Always dribble the basketball in a crouched position.
2. Square up, facing the basket while picking up the dribble.
3. Get the ball in shooting position while jumping straight up into your midjump, propelling the ball in an arc into the basket.
4. Now implement all components of the art of shooting.
5. For starters, shoot one hundred to two hundred shots three times a week. Advanced players, shoot five hundred to six hundred shots three times a week.
6. Remember, your goal is to shoot the perfect shot—nothing but net.
7. If it is not nothing but net, apply the components of the art of shooting that are lacking.
8. Remember, the NBA Follow-through: 1. **N**inety-degree angle (elbow), 2. **B**ackspin, 3. **A**rc, 4. **F**ollow-through.

The Proof Is in the Pudding

I remember King asking me to help him be the best guard in the country. I asked him if he was willing to pay the price to be the best. He did not just say yes, but he demonstrated this by his character, discipline, and work ethic.

He really believes that laziness pays off now, but hard work pays off in the future. His prescriptive plan of attack is no cakewalk. As he shoots thousands of perfect jump shots and thousands of perfect free throws, he is automatically applying the NBA Follow-through. His desired result is the perfect shot, nothing but net. If the ball touches the rim and goes in, King is trained to make the necessary adjustments. During his senior year at his high school, Triple A Academy, King proved that his numbers are not just the best in the state of Texas but also in the country. Due to the training techniques, many adjustments were made throughout the year. Is he the best guard in the country? Maybe not. But you show me a guard with better numbers. My friend once said, "Numbers don't lie, but people do." According to Max Preps, here are King's 2015 statistics in twenty-seven games:

32.1 points/game
16 shots/game
7.7 rebounds/game
4.7 steals/game
3.6 assists/game
76 percent = 2 point FG percent
49 percent = 3P percent
2.0 pps (points per shot)
65 percent = FG percent
86 percent = FT percent
7 *games scored 40+* points
1 game 51 points scored

Max Preps Ranking Amongst Top Twenty-Five Scorers in the Country

76 percent = 2FG%   (#1 in the country)
49 percent = 3P FG%   (#1 in the country)
2.0 pps   (#1 in the country)

65 percent = FG%   (# 2 in the country)
86 percent = FT%   (#3 in the country)

In conclusion, knowing the character of King LeRoy McClure, these numbers do not mean anything to him. He will keep working on his game because he wants to be the best guard in the country. The prize is not given to the swift or the strong but to the one who perseveres.

Chapter 8 Summary

1. One way to improve your shot is to start from the free-throw line. It is always fifteen feet from the basket, and it is free.
2. A perfect shot is the same as "nothing but net." Shoot for Excellence.
3. Do not settle for a made basket unless it hits nothing but net.
4. Settling for a made basket while hitting the rim is like settling for a 90 percent in the classroom when you are able to make a 100 percent.
5. Strive for perfection every time. Make adjustments until you hit nothing but net.
6. **NBA Follow Through –Four Components of Shooting:**
   1) **N**inety degree angle (elbow)
   2) **B**ackspin
   3) **A**rc
   4) **F**ollow through
7. "Whatever is true, whatever is noble, whatever is right, whatever is pure, whatever is lovely, whatever is admirable, if anything is *excellent* or praiseworthy, think about such things." Philippians. 4:9

About the Author

Leroy McClure Jr. was concerned about the high illiteracy and drop-out rates in the African American community. McClure's vision from God became clear when he discovered his brother, Sam, was dyslexic while working with dyslexic children at a private school for students with learning differences.

After learning a specialized reading program, McClure joined the advocacy efforts by creating the FOCUS Centre of Learning, Inc. He is the only African American male Certified Academic Language Therapist in the country.

He has more than twenty-five years of experience in working with children with dyslexia, ADD, and other learning difficulties. He also coached for a private school and hosted basketball clinics for hundreds of children in the Dallas–Fort Worth metropolitan area.

McClure knows firsthand that reading is the gateway to college and/or the world of work. He had a desire to train teachers to work with struggling students far beyond the classrooms at several private schools. His new passion of helping teachers to train students using a multi-sensory teaching approach launched the creation of an innovative charter school for students from pre-K through twelfth grade. He became the Founder/CEO/Superintendent for FOCUS Learning Academy, Inc. with two schools called FOCUS Learning Academy and Triple A Academy.

In 1999, FOCUS Learning Academy opened its doors to one hundred students in kindergarten through sixth grade at a charter school in Dallas. By 2010, the school was up to eighth grade, added a pre-K age 4-year-old program and opened Triple A Academy, the high school cluster starting with ninth and scaling up to twelfth grade. The entire school serves approximately one thousand students with at least one hundred employees.

McClure has a strong academic program combined with a top-notch sports program as part of his repertoire of services. In fact, the very first year of Triple A Academy's membership with the University Scholastic League (UIL), the high-school boys' varsity basketball team became the first charter school team in the history of the state of Texas to win a state championship. His son, King, was one of the starting guards for the 2012–2013 Triple A Stallions team.

McClure graduated from Conway High School in Conway, Arkansas, in 1978 with academic honors and All-State basketball honors.

He received special honors at Richland Community College in Dallas. After two years of studies and basketball at Richland, he traveled 1,100 miles to finish a four-year opportunity of playing basketball and completing his studies in computer engineering at Mayville State University (MSU) in Mayville, North Dakota. While red-shirted at MSU, he was able to compete in a semi-professional basketball league without jeopardizing his basketball eligibility. In 1983, McClure received a computer analyst degree from MSU.

McClure serves as the chairman of the Deacon Board at Ovilla Road Baptist Church, where he attends church. He and his wife, Yvette, live in Ovilla, Texas, and has four children, two adults and two children who attend Triple A Academy.

Made in the USA
San Bernardino, CA
04 July 2015